Ian M Fra

Stories and Prayers for Children

ILLUSTRATED BY MILES FORDE

SAINT ANDREW PRESS

For Laura and Friends

Special thanks to John Henderson for collaboration.

First published in 2000 by
SAINT ANDREW PRESS
BOARD of COMMUNICATION
CHURCH of SCOTLAND
121 George Street, Edinburgh EH2 4YN

ISBN 0 7152 0773 3

British Library Cataloguing in Publication Data
A catalogue record for this book
is available from the British Library.
Printed by Bell & Bain Ltd., Glasgow

Thanks to the Drummond Trust c/o Hill & Robb, 3 Pitt Terrace, Stirling

and to Stirling Council for financial contributions.

Contents

Introduction

The stories, prayers and questions in this small book are designed to encourage children from an early age to care for our planet and its inhabitants.

They take account not only of our environment and of other living things but also of ways in which we should relate sensitively to one another and seek ways of justice and peace to make life on earth a blessing.

Although the stories progress, by and large, from younger to older children, the reader or story teller should feel free to use them in any order and adapt whichever one is chosen to the age group addressed on that particular occasion.

For example, eight-year-olds might not be prepared to admit that the stories of Huffity-puff and Teddy appeal to them... but they could still be involved if the approach were: 'Listen to this story and share this prayer: then we'll discuss whether we think some of the "wee ones" would get the point.' Incidentally they would get the point themselves!

Prayers might be photocopied and distributed on sheets amongst the children or screened from acetates on an overhead projector. In these ways children could be encouraged to participate actively by each speaking a sentence or by making a creative response.

The questions posed after each story can be dealt with in a number of ways too. A time for private thoughts and making a few notes before discussion may be a chosen method on some occasions while at other times immediate discussion may be more appropriate.

On the other hand if teachers have opportunities to take school assemblies, or are looking for source material for classroom drama lessons, they may find some of the stories suitable for dramatic presentation by a class accompanied by a narrator. As well as being great fun for the 'actors' and 'audience', it is possible that learning from the experience can be greater when such drama as a lively visual aid is used to complement the written and spoken word.

Finally it is hoped that the stories and their dramatic potential, the prayers and the questions may encourage parents and teachers to try to make up other stories, prayers and questions of their own (whatever their faith).

Huffity-puff

'Why did they call Jesus "Immanuel"?' asked Derek.

'It means, "God with us",' said his mum.

'But why did they give him that name?' persisted Derek.

'I'm in the middle of baking, can't you see?' said his mum. 'But once these scones are in the oven, I'll tell you a story.'

Derek waited impatiently. At last his mum washed her floury hands and sat down.

'You know from pictures in books and from what you have seen on television that trains once upon a time worked by steam?'

Derek nodded.

'Well, it was at that time that this story takes place.'

There was once a little engine called Huffity-puff who puffed and rattled and chuntered, taking wagons here and there in a goods yard at a station at the foot of a mountain in Wales. He seemed to be perfectly happy. But there were times when he would let off steam in a long 'Sh…h…h…h…h…' Chuffer the big engine and Ted his engine driver knew then that Huffity-puff was looking up the mountain, longing to go where the big engines went.

Then the big day came! The stationmaster, Mr Evans, came to him and said: 'Huffity-puff, we're short of engines today. You'll need to take the people up to the mountain villages.' Huffity-puff was pleased. Oh, how pleased and proud he was to be asked!

So off he went. 'Huffity-puff, huffity-puff, huffity-puff...' without a care in the world. He took the passengers safely to the first village, then the second. After that the slope became much steeper. Huffity-puff had to work hard: 'Huffity ... puff, ... huffity ... puff, ... huffity ... puff': then 'Choo' as the engine stopped. Slowly and silently he started to roll backwards until his driver Sam managed to get the brakes on. There was nothing for it but to put the engine in reverse and carefully shunt the carriages back down to the second village and let the passengers get off. There they had to wait, annoyed and impatient, for the next train up the mountain.

Huffity-puff had to go back to work with the wagons in the goods-yard at the foot of the mountain. Every now and then he would stop and sigh, letting off steam: 'Sh...h...h...h...h...h'. But now it was a hopeless sigh. He would never be able to take people up the mountain. But he hadn't noticed Sam and Ted having a quiet word with Mr Evans the stationmaster.

A few days later Mr Evans came to speak with him again. 'I want you to go to the mountain villages Huffity-puff. I'll put on one less carriage. You'll manage the climb this time.'

Huffity-puff was pleased but very nervous when, after Sam got his steam up, they chugged out of the station. They reached the second village without much trouble. Then came the steep bit. Although Huffity-puff had less weight to pull this time, it was still hard, hard work. The effort he had to put in was so great that even going more and more slowly he was afraid that he might have to give up.

'Huffity … puff, Huffity … puff, Huffity … puff.'

Then just when it seemed that all was lost, he felt new strength coming into him. 'Huffity-puff, huffity-puff, huffity-puff,' he went cheerfully and strongly and pulled the carriages easily from station to station right to the last village at the top of the mountain. He was as proud as punch as he watched the last passengers getting off the train. Then something caught his attention. There were windows right down the platform buildings and they acted like mirrors. "Who's that at the back of my train?' he wondered as he caught sight of something behind the guard's van. 'It's Chuffer!'

Back at his old job in the yard, Huffity-puff was glad to have climbed the mountain, but, as soon as he could, he said to Chuffer, 'It was your strength, not mine, that got us up there, wasn't it?'

'Not true', said Chuffer. 'You did your best. It was when your strength and mine were linked together that we succeeded.'

'That's why Jesus is called Immanuel,' said Derek's mum. 'He doesn't do everything instead of us. Nor does he leave us to go it alone. He is God with us. He joins his strength and power to ours. Then we can do what would be beyond us.'

Prayer:
Lord God,
Our planet is so big !
Yet you put it in our care.
We feel like a wee train faced with a big mountain to climb.
So thank you for Jesus Christ who is willing to add his strength
to our own.
Amen.

Question:
In caring for planet earth what are 'the steepest hills to climb',
the most difficult things to deal with?

Song

Tune: 'Twinkle, twinkle little star...'

God, you're great who made the earth,
brought the stars in space to birth,
shaped the mountain, valley, plain,
thought up sunshine, frost and rain,
fashioned creatures great and small,
trusted us to care for all.

Though we bear your likeness true
we have not been true to you:
your great giving we abuse
turn things to a selfish use:
war, pollution, greed and dearth
scar the face of planet earth.

Lord, forgive us, make us new
guiding us to life that's true.
Grant that creatures, plants and trees
find we don't do as we please
but, as those who've learned your grace,
act as carers in your place.

Bessie

Bessie the Bus was a great favourite with passengers who moved around the countryside and went into town for their weekly shopping. She was nothing much to look at, but she had a heart of gold. I wonder if you know the kind of lady who throws on any kind of clothes in the morning and sticks any kind of hat on her head; who will sit down with children, really listen to them, give them her full attention. Bessie was a bit like that.

Alf, her driver, did not know what to make of her at first. He would halt the bus at a stop. When it was time to move on, he would find on the odd occasion that Bessie would not budge, however hard he pressed the accelerator and worked the clutch and gear lever. In time he learned to look around. Then he might see old Mrs Smith, whose rheumatism was bad that day, hobbling along to the bus stop more slowly than usual; or Mr and Mrs Hendry, held back by the number of small children who had to be washed and dressed. Once they were all aboard, Bessie was ready to move off.

That was why the passengers treated Bessie almost as one of the family. It was not her looks which attracted them. On one occasion she had slid on black ice. To save injury to the passengers she had edged along a wall till she stopped safely. She had suffered scrapes all along one side as a result. The bus company was always intending to repair the damage, but there always seemed to be more urgent claims on the money they had in hand. Nor did the cleaners look after her as they should have.

As long as her passengers were comfortable and safe, Bessie did not really mind. They, in turn, showed their affection. When they left at the end of their journeys, they might say, 'Thank you,' to Alf, but they would also pat Bessie's bonnet and say, 'Well done, Bessie!'

There came the Week for a Sustainable Planet, and with it, the Great Inspection. All the transport in the area was checked and given a rating. The results were posted up in public places including the Bus Station. Anxiously Bessie turned headlight eyes to scan the lists.

The first was headed, 'Appearance'. At the top of the list came flash cars on which their owners lavished much care. Then came the more ordinary cars and some vans and lorries which were well looked after. Bessie let her headlight eyes move down, looking for her own name, till… there it was, at the very foot. Over against it was the comment of the judges: 'Damaged coachwork and scratched paintwork not attended to. Cleaning provision poor'. A big tear rolled down from her windscreen wipers.

She was about to turn away, sad and sorrowful, when she noticed the list headed, 'Community Care'. Worried, she glanced at the foot of the list. It was a relief – she was not there! That space was occupied by the flash cars which used up too much petrol to transport too few people. Timidly she looked further up. She was not there either! Those places were occupied by lorries and vans which belched oily smoke into the atmosphere.

She began to wonder if she had been missed out altogether! But still her headlight eyes moved up till, wonder of wonders, she saw her own name at the top of the list! Alongside was the comment of the judges: 'Bessie carries more people using less energy than any other vehicle we have inspected. She contributes greatly to the sustainability of our life on planet earth.'

At that moment a crowd of children came up to look at the lists. When they saw Bessie's name and the judges' verdict they made a happy circle round her, singing:

'Bessie the bus –
Without any fuss
When it comes to the crunch
You're the best of the bunch.'

Prayer:
Lord God,
The energy in our bodies and energies locked away in our
planet earth enable us to bring life forward from day to day.
Help us to use energy well, not use more than our share:
and help us to choose ways of moving from place to place
which do not pollute our planet.
Amen.

Question:
Can you think of other means of transport which waste energy; or of machines which could be made to work more efficiently with some other form of energy whose use in the long term would do less damage to our planet?

Teddy

There was great excitement in the Toy Cupboard. It was Belinda, the wooden doll's birthday. Sailor Boy could hardly stand still. He danced a jig all over the shelf on which the children placed him when they had finished playing. Squeaker the mouse was beside himself with excitement too. 'Yeep, yeep,' he squeaked, 'yeep, yeep,' and if the children had been around they would surely have heard the sounds.

Belinda herself was lost in a dream. What kind of cake would her friends have prepared? Would the icing be white or pink? How many candles would there be – had the other toys guessed her age correctly or had she still managed to keep that a secret? As for Teddy – he was not bothered whether the icing was white or pink. It was the cake he longed for and other goodies to eat. His tummy was telling him that it was high time that he filled it up again.

But they had to wait for their special guest, Froggie. As the minutes ticked by they grew anxious. It was winter and snow had fallen during the night. They hoped and hoped that everything was all right. Teddy's tummy was becoming more and more demanding and he was just about to say, 'Let's start and Froggie can join us later,' when a snowbird arrived, perching on the knob of the cupboard door and speaking through the keyhole. 'Froggie has asked me to come to tell you that he is stuck in a snowdrift up to the waist and needs to be rescued.' And off went the snowbird, his message safely delivered.

Belinda immediately took charge. 'We must all pray as hard as we can that Froggie will be rescued,' she said. They all got down to praying. After some time, Belinda took a peep through a crack in her fingers. There was no sign of Teddy. The Toy Cupboard door was slightly open. 'Oh that Teddy,' she said to herself. 'All he thinks of is food. He can't keep his mind on praying. Poor Froggie may stay trapped for ever and ever. The rest of us will have to pray all the harder to make up for Teddy.'

After a bit they heard squishy-squashy footsteps approaching. Who squeezed in at the cupboard door but Froggie! Their joy knew no bounds. They hugged one another, and jumped around in great delight.

Behind Froggie came Teddy.

Belinda immediately started to scold him. 'Where have you been? All this time we have been praying hard that Froggie might get free and you gave up and went away. It is a wonder that he was able to join the party.'

'Well,' said Teddy. 'It was like this. I prayed to God that Froggie would get free; and God said to me, "Teddy, there's a spade on the lower shelf." So I got it and went out and found him and dug him out.'

'What's more,' said Froggie, 'the snow was so packed and dangerous that he might have become trapped himself. Good old Teddy!'

Putting his hands above his head, Froggie danced in circles round the shelf shouting with glee. 'Pray and dare! Pray and dare! It's no good praying without daring. Pray and dare like Teddy Bear!'

Prayer:
Lord God,
You took a risk when you gave us charge of this earth.
We give thanks for your trust that we would care for it.
Help us, we pray, so that we may see more and more clearly
how all life can be marked by joy and justice, love and care for others.
When there is something we ourselves must do, give us your
spirit to enable us to get up and do it.
Amen.

Question:
What can we do ourselves to care for planet earth and to free people who are in some way trapped?

Tracey

Tracey the Turtle lived in Lake Tanganyika in Africa. It is a huge lake, its borders touching four countries. It is also the second deepest lake in the world. Tracey felt very small in its vastness.

One day she stuck her head above the waters and saw a giraffe on the lake-shore. 'What a lovely long neck,' she thought to herself. 'Here am I in this huge lake. When I put my head above the water I can only see a tiny bit of it. But a giraffe must be able to see for miles and miles. I wish I were a giraffe and not a turtle!'

So she prayed, 'God, please make me into a giraffe!' But God did not change her into a giraffe.

Another day Tracey stuck her head above the waters and there, at the lakeside, having a drink, was a lion. Tracey knew that lions and lionesses were kings and queens of the jungle. 'Here am I, so small,' she thought. 'No one ever bothers about me or thinks that I am important. Lions are so majestic, they hold their heads so proudly. Other animals look up to them and live in fear of them. I wish I were a lion and not a turtle!'

So she prayed, 'God, please make me into a lion!' But God did not change her into a lion.

Then, one day, it was a rhinoceros that Tracey saw at the lakeside. She admired its body which seemed to be armour-plated all over. It looked so strong! When it went back into the jungle, nothing could stop it. It carved a road through the prickliest, thorniest bushes, and all other animals kept out of its

way. Tracey sighed, 'I have a shell to protect me too. But I am small, not big and strong like a rhino. I wish I were a rhino and not a turtle!'

So she prayed, 'God, please make me a rhinoceros!' But God did not change her into a rhinoceros.

The day Tracey will never forget was one when there were sounds of crackling and a great wind and lots of smoke. During the night the lake had been lit up by a glare of yellow and orange and red light. As Tracey looked, a forest fire swept through the trees right to the lakeside. There was not a giraffe, or a lion, or a rhino in sight. They had been driven away before the flames and had been forced to leave their homes to find some place which the fire could not reach.

'If I were a giraffe, I would lose my home,' said Tracey.

'If I were a lion, I would lose my home,' said Tracey.

'If I were a rhino, I would lose my home,' said Tracey.

I wonder if you could guess the prayer she prayed then? It was this:

'God, please answer my prayers by giving me what is good for me and for the world, whether that is what I ask for or not.'

She swam down to the cool depths of the lake. As she swam she said to herself:

'Turtles are needed every bit as much as giraffes or lions or rhinos.'

Prayer:
Lord God,
You knew what you were doing when you made the world and all its living creatures. You rejoiced to see the variety and abundance of life.
Help us make the most of the special kind of life you have given to each one of us. May our lives praise you!
You know what is best for us. Whatever we ask for in prayer, please notice what lies behind what we ask, and give us what is best for ourselves and for the world.
Amen.

Question:
What different kinds of gifts are needed to care for planet earth and its people?

Abdul

Abdul had been lying in the sun in the grass. He might have dozed off. At any rate he was lying quite still. Then he heard voices. Some argument was taking place. He sat up. The voices stopped. There was no sign of anyone around.

Puzzled and sleepy, he lay back down in the grass. He kept perfectly quiet.

After some time he heard the voices again. Abdul then realised that it was the vegetables arguing amongst themselves! The local Flower Show had just taken place. There the best vegetables had been awarded prizes. The vegetables in Abdul's garden were arguing about the type of vegetable among them which deserved to be called Chief Vegetable of All.

'Look at me!' said the cabbage. 'Look at my lovely shape, rounded to a point, my leaves beautifully balanced.'

'But you are all for show,' said the carrot. 'I hide my beauty beneath the ground till I am needed to feed people.'

'None of you can compare with me,' said the Brussels sprout plant. 'None of you have the height and grace as well as produce good food. Look at the lovely flounces my leaves make.'

'I am a perfect round,' said the beetroot.

'No wonder you look red ashamed,' said the parsnip. 'Compare yourself with my golden purity!'

So on and on they argued. But the leek took no part. At last they turned to it.

'Have you no word to say for yourself, old half-and-half,

half in the ground, and half above it?' they teased.

'There's nothing outstanding about me,' said the leek.

'Come on,' they said. 'We have all spoken of special things backing our claim to be Chief Vegetable of All. You must have something good to say about yourself.'

'Well there's just one thing,' said the leek at last. 'I keep growing through the winter.'

A hush fell on the company. There was a very long silence. Then a voice said: 'We take advantage of the summer sun and rain. Then we die back or have to be taken indoors for protection. To keep growing through the winter is a very special thing.'

Then all of them said: 'The leek gets the crown. The leek is Chief Vegetable of All. To be able to grow through the winter is best of all.'

16

Prayer:
God the Lord,
We give you thanks for vegetables, the look of them,
the shape of them, the taste of them. They give us health.
We give thanks for those who grow them and
sell them and cook them.
We give thanks also for people who, when they face difficult
times, still keep 'growing through the winter'.
Forgive us if we fail you when the sun stops shining.
Amen.

Questions:
How do vegetables give us health? Do you eat your share?

Willie

Willie the Wheelie-Bin was fed up. It was all right for Wilma. She was a younger, fresher, shinier wheelie-bin. In the school grounds she was far better placed for getting the attention of pupils and teachers. She was situated between the main school door and the playground. Willie was at the main gate. Not only did Willie have few of the school community using him, but when people in neighbouring houses had an overflow of their own rubbish they stuffed it all into Willie. All this gave Willie indigestion!

Some boys and girls at the school were fed up too. They were keen on football. They had asked the headteacher to put up goalposts in the playground. 'We don't want just to kick a ball around,' they pleaded. 'To get better at scoring and saving goals we need to learn to shoot at a decent target and we would only need one set of goalposts for that. They won't take up too much room.' But the headteacher said that the playground had to be kept for all of the children of the school, playing all kinds of games. Yes, a kick-about in the playground was a good enough way for them to learn football skills meantime, but - no goalposts!

A member of the local Council, who had special responsibility for the school, dropped in there from time to time without warning. One day he arrived after the children had been in a huddle wondering what to do about goalposts. 'I know,' said Elinor. 'Let's use the wheelie-bins.'

'Good idea,' said Tom. 'They're not picked up until tomorrow, so they'll be full, and make strong posts.' So Willie and Wilma were wheeled into position. They made excellent goal-posts and could be removed when they were not needed. When the Councillor arrived and saw the solution the children had worked out, he was very taken with it and watched their practice with interest.

Now Tom just happened to be a bit bigger than the others and had a very strong shot in his left foot. Rosie had kicked for goal, the goalie punched it out, Tom took the ball on the drop. Bang! It hit Willie so hard in his top section that it knocked him over. His lid flew open and out spilled the contents. The Councillor came over to have a look. Bottles, newspapers, plastic lay jumbled together. 'With all that lot inside him,' chuckled the Councillor, 'Willie must have had a sore tummy' – not knowing how near the mark he was! 'We must do better than this,' he added.

Near the school gate you will now find separate containers which the Council provided for bottles and newspapers. Willie is still not noticed so much as Wilma. But he's a happier wheelie-bin. His indigestion has gone.

Prayer:
Lord God,
Teach us to value the things we need in order to live each day
and to find different uses for what we might throw away
so that nothing is wasted which could be recycled:
for you have met our needs generously
and we should use your gifts thoughtfully.
Amen.

Question:
Why is recycling important for life on Planet Earth?

David

David lived in the country. Birds fascinated him, especially blue tits and great tits, coal tits, willow tits and, down on the boggy ground where the river spilled over its banks, marsh tits. He loved to watch them hopping through the hedges round the garden, catching flying insects both for themselves and for the young ones at nesting times. The nests were of moss, grass, hair (where horses had rubbed against fences), wool (where sheep had gone under wire) and feathers. You could find nests in a hole in a tree or wall, even at times in the ground.

One day, David found that a pair of great tits had begun to build a nest in the letter-box of the house! When the family

gathered together for their evening meal, they discussed what to do. We'll leave them, it was decided, and tell postie to leave letters in the porch instead.

'But once the young ones have gone,' said David, 'they may well come back, next year!'

'Well,' said his dad, 'they can't occupy our letter-box for ever. We will clean out the nest when it is no longer needed. But I'll tell you what you can do, David. You can make a nesting box with a hole just the right size for the tits to enter, and put it on a post in the garden near the letter-box. They might make that their home next year.'

And so they did. David was pleased. He had set the nesting box so that the hole faced north, the way tit families like it, and in due course the tits had brought up their youngsters in it. However, a year or two later the tits did not come back to the nesting box.

'What's wrong?' said David.

His mum answered: 'I think I know. Remember that long frost we had at the beginning of the year, well into May? It killed off flying insects on which tits depend for food. Don't you remember the nests in which we found dead fledgelings? There just was not enough food to keep them alive. So there are fewer tits, and that means less demand for nesting places.'

A few years later, tits almost disappeared from the area.

'What's wrong this time?' said David. 'We haven't had a big frost!'

'No,' said his dad. 'But look at what has been happening in the fields here roundabout the house. Hedges have been ripped out. Fields have been put together. Pesticides have been sprayed over crops. Tits do not have the hedges they love to hop about in. Flying insects are killed by the sprays so that food for the young birds is very scarce. Birds themselves have been poisoned. We're meant to look after the earth – fields, plants and hedges, birds and beasts. When we don't do that we let God down and let our planet suffer. We have to live differently and care for God's creatures.'

Prayer:
Lord God, we praise you for the gifts of the earth, for the wild areas and the places on which we grow food.
We praise you for other living creatures which share the planet with us.
Help us to know the difference between destructive forces which are beyond our control, like frost, and those which we can control.
Help us to stop spoiling the earth and preventing other living creatures from sharing it with us.
We ask it in Jesus' name.
Amen.

Question:
What hurts the life of animals and birds, that you have noticed?

Alice and Andrew

Alice and Andrew were twins. They did almost everything
together. Their parents were keen gardeners and had quite a
large garden. When the weather was fine they liked to work as a
team, Alice and Andrew helping where they could. From time to
time the twins also visited Old Tom, who had an allotment
nearby. It seemed that he knew everything there was to know
about gardening. They would sit at his feet and would learn what
made good soil, how and when seeds should be planted, how to
tend and care for them, when to harvest crops and how to store
them. By the time they were seven years old they knew a great
deal about flowers and vegetables.

It was then that Old Tom made his suggestion. Why not ask
their parents for a bit of the family garden which would become
their own to look after, to grow what they wanted? The children
did ask, and their dad and mum talked it over. They decided that
they were prepared to give the children a bit of land on one
condition. They had to learn the cost of gardening, and buy out
of their pocket money or make with their own hands whatever
was needed to do the work successfully.

'We will put up a wired fence to mark off the bit of land
which will be yours. We will also pay for the seeds you need.
Otherwise you are on your own,' they said.

Alice and Andrew were delighted. They dug over the land,
ready for planting. They sowed the seed at the right time,
watched with pleasure as the plants grew, tended and cared for

them, and then transplanted them when they were strong enough to grow by themselves.

From time to time they would sit down and think about what they were doing. 'Are we making the best use of our bit of land?' asked Alice. 'Are we thinking ahead to the next year too?' asked Andrew.

Alice had an idea. 'We can't afford to buy supports for peas,' she said, 'but mum and dad have promised to buy seed for us. We can get twigs to support them in the first stages and then grow them up the fence.'

'Good idea,' said Andrew.

Andrew was worried as he thought far ahead. How could the soil be kept fertile? 'I wonder', said Alice, 'if the two wooden boxes which the new mower and the electrical digger arrived in would be of use to us and whether mum and dad would let us have them.'

'Let's ask Old Tom what he thinks,' said Andrew, and off they went to talk with their friend. 'We know that we could buy fertilizer but we have other things to spend our money on. Is there some less expensive way to keep the soil in good trim for next year?' At that point they mentioned the two wooden boxes which were lying at the back door. Tom asked about their size and the kind of strips of wood they were made of.

'One of these,' he said, 'might just make a composting box. I live by myself,' he went on, 'and there is not much waste matter for me to compost. But there are four of you. The outer leaves of vegetables and any vegetables you don't need can be recycled and provide fertilizer for all the years ahead. Even the stems will make compost if they are well smashed up beforehand.'

He showed them how to take off every second strip of wood from the box to provide air. That included the bottom of the box which had to be covered with a small spare piece of wire netting. Into this box went all the waste – and even soft cardboard which they saved from parcels. Every now and again they turned the waste over in the box and added some soil. They also made sure that it was kept damp. The result was that, by autumn, they had enough compost to dig in for the year to come.

All this time, Andrew was wondering what might be done with the other box, which was longer than the first but not as broad. Quite often he used it as a bench in the tool shed. He was passing the local shop one day when he saw men unloading a delivery van. They were carrying out a frame with trays on which pot plants could be placed at different levels. The frame was wrapped in a plastic cover and he immediately asked the shopkeeper what he did with the cover. 'I put it in the bin,' was the reply. 'Please then may I have it instead,' said Andrew. 'Certainly,' said the shopkeeper.

When he got home Andrew took off the lid and base of the remaining box, leaving only the sides. When he wrapped the plastic round what remained, he and Alice had their own home-made cold frame! Next year they would be able to bring forward plants from seeds earlier than before, because the frame would protect them from cold winds and frost.

Prayer:
Lord God,
You have provided so much to make life on earth interesting; and to supply our needs.
Enable us, we pray, to use our imagination to make the best use of what is already to hand.
Amen.

Question:
Think: What kind of things, treated as waste, can be put to a different use, so that we do not drain the planet of its resources unnecessarily?

Douglas and Peter

Douglas had a toy van which was his pride and joy. It went 'vroom, vroom' when, holding it tightly, he ran its wheels a few times along the floor. Then when he let it go it took off and travelled a fair distance before stopping.

One day his cousin Peter came to stay with the family for a week or so. He was a few years older than Douglas and his great hobby was constructing models from assembly kits. He would work carefully with the different pieces, glue them together, and produce a ship or an aeroplane where you could not see any of the joins. Friends and neighbours greatly admired his work.

Douglas had been keen to show off his favourite van, so he said to Peter, 'Come on upstairs to the landing and see how my van works.' Up they went and Douglas wound up the engine in the usual way and then let it go across the carpet. It started beautifully. But they had not noticed a fold in the carpet a few yards down the landing. When the van bumped into the fold, it turned at right angles, went straight between two of the landing railings, fell to the floor below and lay there smashed.

Douglas could hardly keep back his tears. Peter noticed this and said quickly, 'I know about cars; I'll mend it for you.' He picked up the wrecked car, took it to the garage workbench and started to repair it.

When he took it back to Douglas, it looked as good as new. Douglas thanked him and tried it out along the kitchen floor. Nothing happened! The back wheels which had fallen off in the crash were still not turning. 'How did you mend them?' asked Douglas.

'I glued them on,' said Peter.

'But they need to be fixed to the back axle which revs up the engine, or the motor can't carry the van forward,' said Douglas.

'Oh, I see,' said Peter. 'Let's go together this time and try to fix it.'

Even after they had unglued the wheels and re-attached them to the axle, the engine would not work. 'It must have been damaged in the fall,' said Peter. 'I know that kind of engine. I'll work on it and this time I won't use glue!'

This time when he brought it back to the kitchen it gave its old 'vroom, vroom' and shot off across the floor as before. Unfortunately this time it hit the leg of a chair and its bonnet fell off. 'That's where you should have used glue,' laughed a happy Douglas, and after they had done so, the van not only ran well but looked good too.

That night, before he went to sleep, Peter thought about the van and what had happened. 'To put things right, you have to put everything right,' he said to himself. And at that moment, what he had heard in a geography lesson at school became clearer than before.

The teacher had shown them a map of Africa highlighting Mozambique, a country in the south of the continent. He had told them how it had been invaded, crops, houses and people destroyed, a fertile land brought to ruin. To deal with the devastation, money had been borrowed from banks. This had meant that much of the country's tiny earnings had been needed to try to repay the interest on the loan. All this did was to increase poverty and leave them with a debt which was so great that it could never be paid off, ever. On the top of all this, there have since been devastating floods.

The teacher then asked the pupils to try to picture a boy or girl in a village in Mozambique and think of how they themselves might help such a child.

At first the class thought of putting aside some pocket money to send to him or her. Then some said, 'But if we picked out one child, that would make him or her privileged, and other children who didn't get any such help would feel even worse off than before.'

At that point the teacher told them of Plan International, where contact could be made personally with one child but the whole village benefited from the clean water, medical care and schooling which the money provided. They all thought that this was a much better way of helping. 'What else?' said the teacher.

The class could not think of anything else – till one bright girl suggested that the whole country needed to be freed from debt or it would just sink lower and lower.

'Yes,' said Peter to himself drowsily, 'to put things right, you have to put everything right.'

Prayer:
Lord God,
We are one human family. Where some of the family have suffered, and a good life has been destroyed, help us to do what we can to put things right – remembering all the things that need to be put right.
Amen.

Question:
How can people who are well-off help those who are poor without taking away their dignity?

The Armstrong Family

The Armstrong family had fishing in their blood. Eric's earliest years were spent at a seaport. His Uncle John owned a trawler. Later Eric's parents moved inland, but a river flowed past at the foot of their garden and Eric learned freshwater angling. Not too far away was a loch, stocked with trout. There Eric won several competitions with his catches. Imagine his delight when he got a junior salmon rod for his tenth birthday!

By that time he had learned many of the secrets of the river: the deep pools with rocks under which fish hid out of sight; the habits of salmon at spawning time when they sailed over the falls to lay eggs in its upper reaches; the different flies to use when the water was low or just after a spate. Most days he went fishing after school, and always at weekends.

One day Uncle John, who owned the trawler, came visiting. Their conversation was all about fish. Eric said to him: 'I can catch fish in the loch, no problem, but I don't seem to have the knack of catching salmon in the river.'

'Wild salmon are getting scarce,' said his uncle. 'The problem might not be your lack of skill but that salmon are not there in the numbers they used to be. That is the case with the sea as well. I am being forced to give up fishing and sell my trawler, not because I am too old but because the sea is getting over-fished.'

'I can't imagine a fishing fleet without an Armstrong in it!' said Eric.

'Well, we must all be ready for changes if we are destroying the earth's bounty when we should be using it carefully and leaving a better situation for our children,' said Uncle John. 'Over many years fishing boats have been getting bigger and nets have been getting smaller. The authorities have banned the worst nets now, but too many immature fish have already been caught – and either thrown back dead into the sea or sold to fish-meal factories. It cannot go on like this. Fish stocks need a chance to recover.

'I don't want to leave the sea. But I think too highly of the sea and what it provides to rob it of more than we need to live on – and that's what is happening.'

Prayer:
Lord God,
Make us content with enough to live on, no more,
so that other people and our children do not suffer through our thoughtlessness.
May our way of living be a kind of 'thank you' to you for trusting us with a planet so rich in things we need and enjoy.
Amen.

Question:
If you were Uncle John, and fishing was in your blood, how would you react when forced to stop, and why?

Arun

In a distant country lived Arun, a bamboo tree. He was proud of himself, with justice! He grew taller than all the trees around. Up and up he went till he reached about 35 metres high! The secret of his height was this. The area around him was cut in two by a stone ridge. Where Arun stood there was a strong spring of water which ran down the slope to feed rivers further down. Arun had as much water as he needed. So there was no hindrance to his growth.

On the other side of the ridge were fields which had no such water source but needed good rain to thrive. People depended on the crops for their livelihood.

One year the rains failed. Week after week people looked up at the skies longing for a change in the weather. But it appeared as if all the crops would die.

Some of the people who lived on the produce of the fields crossed over the dividing ridge to where Arun stood. They studied the other bamboo trees around, and shook their heads. 'Too small,' they said. They then looked at Arun. 'That's the only one big enough,' they decided. 'We'll have to cut him down.'

Arun was horrified. But then it looked as if he might be saved after all.

'We think of this tree, Arun, as our friend' said one woman. 'We are very fond of him – he somehow seems part of the family. It would be a sad day if were to lose him.'

'He gives direction to travellers,' said another. 'He stands so

high that they know where they are when they see him and can plan their journey exactly and safely.'

'But what alternative is there?' asked a third voice. Reluctantly they agreed that there was no other option open to them. No other tree would do.

So Arun was cut down.

What do you think the fields-people did?
How would what they had done help them?

First they made sure that the hollow middle was completely clear of pith which might block the passage of water. Then they put one end into the spring of water and the other end over the ridge to the lower fields on the other side.

The water flowed into the fields! The crops revived and went on to produce a good harvest of grain and vegetables.

Arun said to himself: 'I thought I had lost my life, my tall beauty, the sign I was for travellers. Now I have found another kind of life. I provide means for life-giving water to reach places which need it.'

Prayer:
Lord God,
We thank you for water to drink, to bathe in, to play with.
We remember countries where water is scarce and people suffer.
Make our lives like a bamboo pipe so that all people may be able to have enough water which they can drink safely and wash in,
enough water to make the crops grow.
We ask it in Jesus' name.
Amen.

Questions:
What do you want your life to be like? How can it be best made a blessing to others?

Kwame

Sometimes it was a story from the bible which Kwame's mum or dad told or read to him before he went to sleep. One night his mum chose Noah and the Ark.

'It can't be a true story,' said Kwame. 'It says that every living thing was wiped out. Fish are living things. They weren't wiped out.'

'Look more carefully,' said his mum. 'It says everything on dry land died.'

'It says birds too,' persisted Kwame. 'But they could fly above the waters.'

'Not for ever,' said his mum. 'They would need places to perch and rest. When these disappeared under the waves, they would drown. It would be a bit as it was some years ago in China. It seemed to those in charge that sparrows were robbing people of food by eating so much grain at harvest time. So they set up a great din, banging on pots and pans to keep sparrows in the air till they fell dead of exhaustion. (By the way, the sparrows got their own back. The following year crops were destroyed by bugs which the sparrows had previously eaten!) Birds need perches.'

'But was there really a flood and a Noah?' asked Kwame.

'Drainage in the ancient world was very poor,' said his mum. 'That could lead to floods. Also remember that people treated their own surrounding area as the "world" – it was all the world they knew. There might have been that kind of basis for

the tale. But the aim of the story is to waken our imagination so that it gets across to us some truth about life. When Jesus told the story of the Good Samaritan, there might never have been an actual incident on the road between Jerusalem and Jericho just as he described it. But his story is a parable. It teaches us how to live, caring for one another.'

'So what does Noah and the Ark teach us?' asked Kwame.

'We have done such a bad job of caring for the earth and for one another that God would be justified in destroying everything and inventing a different world and people who would take his way more faithfully. But God sticks with this world as it is and with us as we are. Noah and his family are not heroes or angels. They are ordinary folk like us with all their failings. God keeps making a fresh start with the likes of us. Later, remember, Jesus made it clear that God is not on a mission of destruction but a mission of rescue of the world and its people.'

'I've thought of one more thing,' said Kwame yawning. 'I've read of a Christian community in Chile at a time of great drought. The cattle died off as it went on and on. Then the community thought: "God did not mean us to give in to famine, but to fight it." So they kept what animal feed was left for breeding pairs – and built up stock once again when the rains came. The animals went into the ark two by two! I'm glad I thought of that.'

At that he put his head on the pillow and fell fast asleep.

Prayer:
Lord God,
Enable us to find vivid stories to get across to one another
things which matter and which are true to life,
that we might be like Jesus,
whose stories made others think what life was for,
so that they made discoveries about it which were their own.
Amen.

Question:
What do you make of the story of Noah and the Ark?

Amanda

Amanda thought she was a failure.

Other children were good at sport, at reading and writing, at sums, or at doing things in the house or garden. Her mind seemed to work very slowly. Her hand movements were clumsy. She was a friendly lass and was happy at playtimes and holiday times just enjoying herself with others. But whereas her friends were quick in the classroom and at doing tasks outside, she was slow and awkward. When Miss Grant was appointed and became her teacher, she was beginning to lose heart.

The attitude of her parents did not help. One day she had come home across the grass towards the kitchen door. Her mum and dad were sitting in the sun with their backs to her. She realized that they were talking about her. She stayed behind the hedge, out of sight, to hear what they were saying. They thought of her as a loveable child. 'It's just as well,' her dad was saying, 'for she is not likely to make her mark on the world. She's not brainy and she's all thumbs when it comes to practical tasks.' Her mum agreed but went on, 'But, dear, it is being loving that matters most.'

'You're right,' said her dad, 'there's much to be grateful in that.' Amanda crept away in the direction from which she had come so that they did not see her. She was cheered that they appreciated her loving nature. But her heart also sank because they seemed so sure that, otherwise, she was a bit of a failure.

All the children at Amanda's school were asked to do some

work outside the building as well as in the classroom. Spaces in the school garden were shared out. The children could grow in each what they pleased. Amanda was given a little plot.

She thought, 'I don't know anything about gardening. Things won't grow for me. What can I do?' After a bit she decided: 'I'll get the book on gardening from the school library and do exactly what it says. When Miss Grant sees that nothing will grow for me even when I do everything right she will stop asking me to do what I can't.'

That year, Easter was late. Before the holidays, Amanda weeded the ground, dug it and added horse manure from a nearby field. She raked it till the soil on top became smooth and crumbly. Then she took a hoe and made small furrows, about one centimetre deep. She sowed two packets of seed, taking care to space them at the distance shown on the packet. At last she said to herself, 'I've done everything the book says: no one can blame me if nothing grows.' She put the task out of her mind, and enjoyed the Easter holidays.

When school started again, the fun she had had during the holidays with her friends was still uppermost in her mind and she did not go to see what had happened to her bit of garden. It was almost a month after she had planted the seed that Miss Grant stopped her in the corridor and asked how things were coming on in her garden patch. Amanda pretended that she had shown enough interest to keep an eye on it: 'Things just don't grow for me,' she replied.

'That's strange,' said Miss Grant. 'Tell me what you did.' Amanda told her. 'But you have done everything right,' said her teacher. 'It's funny that you have had no success. Come and show me.'

When they came in sight of Amanda's plot, Miss Grant turned to her pupil. 'You said that things would not grow for you. Are my eyes playing tricks?' For there, in neat rows where Amanda had planted seeds were green shoots, all looking very healthy.

'I can't understand it,' said Amanda. 'I'm not a gardener!'

'What is a gardener?' asked her teacher.

'Someone who knows how to make things grow,' said Amanda.

'Then you are a gardener!' said Miss Grant.

She went on: 'Amanda, I've been watching you over the

weeks that I've been here. You don't appreciate yourself enough, and others don't either. The way you tackled your bit of garden shows how carefully and thoughtfully you approach your work. Others may have quicker minds. But you may go further in the end. I'm proud of the way you stick in.'

'I really thought I was born to be a failure,' said Amanda.

'Nobody's born to be a failure,' said Miss Grant. 'Everyone has gifts. The thing is to value them and find the best ways to put them to use.'

Prayer:
Lord God,
Help us not to think too much or too little of ourselves.
May we use the gifts you have given us to make planet earth a better place for all to live in.
Amen.

Question:
What gifts do we value too little in others, and in ourselves?

Bob

Bob the bulldozer would have scratched his head – if he had known which part of him could have been called his head and if his arms had been free instead of fixed on each side of the big shovel at the front. So often he had been playing a part in making roads.

CARING FOR PLANET EARTH

On one occasion people who thought that one road being planned would deprive wild creatures and themselves of countryside which they should be free to enjoy had lain down in front of him. If he had gone forward he would have squashed them. So he had stopped short and refused to budge, protecting them from harm. 'Roads take away space where dragon-flies can play, where squirrels can scamper, where birds can nest, and where people can wander enjoying the countryside. People had a right to say what roads they think are needed and what roads are not,' thought Bob.

What puzzled him was the job he had now been sent to. He had been sent to Ortmoor, a wild place near Orthampton. There was a plan to build a motorway over it. He had gone expecting to do the usual thing – level the ground, push mud out of the way, lay a solid base for road surfacing. Instead he was being asked to help make something like a mud-pie! In place of levelling the ground he had to make holes and humps and hollows. Instead of making good channels for the water he had to get it to ooze all over the place, so that the ground became muddier than ever. It was all the opposite of what he usually did. He wondered, but could not find an answer. What was this all about?

Then one day a family of four came walking by and stopped near where he had been left to spend the night at the end of a working day. 'Isn't it lovely,' said the lady, looking over the mess which Bob had made. 'I'm so glad that our protests forced the Department of Transport to build the road round this place instead of through it.'

'So that's what's happened,' thought Bob to himself. 'There won't be a road here after all. It is some different work that I'm meant to be doing.'

'Have you ever seen a bittern?' broke in Sandy. 'It lives in reed beds. The reed beds here will soon be spreading.'

'There are hardly any waders around now, or lapwings or buzzards. Some time ago there were plenty,' added Rachel.

'I remember those years though you won't,' said their mum. 'But by the time you grow up, more and more birds will have found this place and made a home in it once more. Even the shy bittern may return.'

At that point they looked straight at Bob. 'You're doing a good job,' they said. 'You are giving creatures a little world in which they can live happily,' and they patted his side affectionately before going on their way.

Prayer:
Lord God,
We know that the world is not ours.
It is home for all kinds of living creatures as well.
Teach us to care for them, making sure there are habitats which suit them.
Forgive us that there are habitats which we have destroyed through thoughtlessness or greed.
Teach us what to restore, in order to be fair to all life.
Amen.

Question:
Who should decide what roads are needed and where they should go?

Donald and Elspeth

Donald and Elspeth had very different natures. Brothers and sisters often have. Donald liked to be up and doing. Elspeth liked nothing better than to get away from everyone else into a corner with a book. At school it was Elspeth who got good marks. Donald could have done quite well if he had tried. It was not that he lacked brains. He just did not apply himself. He could not see the point of a subject such as Maths. Why, he wondered, if

you use your eyes properly and also use your common sense, should you have to work out things on paper. Eye measurement of length, breadth and height can be made on the spot where a job is to be done. Correct angles and the thickness of different materials can be taken into account too. So he did not bother. His classroom work suffered as a result.

One day he came back all excited at an idea which had come to him. There was a big, strong tree in the garden. He would build a tree house!

He saved up pocket money until he could go to the scrapyard with a barrow to buy and bring back the wood he needed. He was also lucky to find some felt covering for the roof, secondhand but still watertight. Once he got nails he was ready to start. After school and at weekends he spent long hours trimming tree branches for a base, and erecting the tree house.

When it was finished, to tell the truth, you could have mistaken it for a higgledy-piggledy pile of sticks! Still it provided shelter. Donald and his friend Tony could spend time among the branches, pretending they were Tarzan of the Apes, with dense jungle around.

One night there was a storm, not a very big storm, but one that was marked by a strong wind. In the morning the tree house was lying around the foot of the tree in bits. It was a cruel blow to Donald. All his work had gone for nothing.

Elspeth saw how downhearted he was and tried to comfort him. 'The wood is still there, none of it is missing,' she said. 'You could make another tree house.'

'What would be the point?' asked Donald. 'If a bad storm blows up, it will just smash that one too.'

'Not if it is well built,' said Elspeth. But seeing that he was still sad and unconvinced, she added, 'And I would be willing to help you.'

Donald brightened at the thought of not having to do the work all over again on his own. 'Right!' he said.

But from the start they had different ideas on how the task should be tackled. Elspeth got out pencil and paper and measuring instruments and made out a plan. Donald shouted over to her: 'If you want to be a real help you should not waste time on that kind of thing. Help me get the wood up there instead.'

'Come and let's talk about it,' said Elspeth.

When he reached her, she went on, 'Look at the wood, Donald. Your nails were not long enough to join the planks securely. We must measure the thickness of the wood and get nails of the right length. The corners of your tree house were not at right angles – that made it easier for the wind to blow it down.

'We must get the angles right. Also we will need to get metal supports to strengthen the corners – a tree house has to stand up to a greater force of wind than anything on the ground, which may be protected by walls and hedges.' She went on, showing where other faults were taken into account on the plans which she had drawn up. Donald was amazed. This sister of his had never tried to build a tree house in her life. Yet she had put her finger on weaknesses which had resulted in the smashing of the first one. Moreover she had all this worked out on paper!

They started again, each learning from the other, each appreciating the other's gifts.

In the end they stood on the ground looking up at what they had built high in the tree, satisfied with their work (which stood up to many storms in the years ahead). Donald gave a little laugh and said: 'I see now that Maths in the classroom and a tree house in the garden are like brother and sister. They need one another for a good job to be done.'

Prayer:

Lord God,

We give thanks for our minds and our hands and for ways in which their different abilities fit together.

We give thanks for schools and teachers who help us to get different kinds of knowledge which fit together in life.

We give thanks for one another.

Help us to find how classroom learning and real life come together to help us to manage life well.

Amen.

Question:

Can you think of times in your life when you have found that 'two minds are better than one' and that 'many hands make better and easier work'?

Sheila

'What would you like for your birthday, Sheila?' her mum asked.

'Oh you know fine what I want,' replied Sheila.

'No, I don't.'

'Well, I want a pony like Alison's.'

'How often do I have to tell you — there's no place to keep a pony here.'

'No, mum, but you could buy a place like Alison's, with a field for a pony.'

Sheila's dad had died and her mum and she were left on their own. Her mum went out every day to work as a lawyer. 'Alison's mum is a lawyer too,' grumbled Susan. 'If she can get a better house, why can't we?'

'I don't get paid as much as she does,' said her mum. 'And there are more important things than money.'

'Nothing is more important than a pony,' said Sheila.

Alison and she were best friends. They had another friend called Lisa, whom they saw less often because she lived in the nearby town.

Before Sheila's birthday arrived, her mum noticed she had become sad and listless. There was something on her mind. But her mum just went quietly about her business, not enquiring, in case it was something which Sheila had to work out for herself, without sharing the problem.

At last Sheila burst out: 'It's not fair!'

'What's not fair?' asked her mum.

It all came out in a rush. Lisa's family had rented a house. The landlord wanted to sell his property for profit. Lisa's family would be put out with nowhere to stay. 'It's not fair,' said Sheila in despair. 'The landlord just wants more money, he doesn't bother about what happens to people as a result. What's more, they can't go to court to fight the order. Since Lisa's dad took ill they have used up all their savings. They can't afford the fees!' She cried hot tears.

'I know,' said her mum. Sheila looked up, surprised.

'You don't have the whole story,' said her mum. 'Lisa's mum came to me, wondering what to do. I work for a Legal Action Group. It seeks to get justice for those who could not afford it otherwise. We will make it possible for the family to go to court. I will fight the case myself for them without charge.'

'Oh, mum,' said Sheila, eyes shining. 'That's marvellous!'

'Look,' said her mum. 'This kind of thing can only be done if I accept much smaller fees than I would get by taking cases which would be better paid. But I think we are given life to care for others. I will never have enough money coming in to pay for a house with a field and a pony – not if I help people like Lisa's family.'

Susan was quiet for a long time. Then she said: 'Whatever you give me for my birthday, mum, don't let it be a pony. Keep working where you are and help people like Lisa's family, please.'

Prayer:
Lord God,
Life is a gift.
We get it to make the world a better place.
Those who find life hard should be able to turn to us for help; and we need them too.
Save us from being selfish.
At the end, may you be able to say to us, 'I trusted you with a life and you used it to bless others. Good for you!'
Amen.

Question:
How can we make sure that everyone, however rich or poor they are, has access to justice?

Jacques, Paul
and Claude

In the village lived three brothers, very different in nature from one another but all known for their wisdom. It was a dry area dependent on a few springs for water. When the water became nasty in its taste and smelled strangely — though it was not poisonous — the brothers were approached for help.

The first brother, Jacques, gathered the village people around him and said to them, 'You realize that there is nothing wrong with the water for supporting life. It enables our crops to grow, it quenches our thirst. The problem is the taste and smell. But we can deal with that by training ourselves to make the best of what we have. We can teach ourselves to get used to the taste, we can hold our noses as we drink. It is up to us to make the best of what we have. Water is still a great gift from God.'

People did as he said. But still they longed for clean refreshing water.

The second brother, Paul, meantime, had taken a sample to be tested in the science department of the university. They found what was causing the bad taste and smell and what was needed to put things right. But the cure was expensive. The brother approached bodies which gave money for good causes. He had to wait until they met to make their decisions, but at last he raised enough for a month's supply of the remedy. The villagers were glad to hear his news. They built a small dam with their own hands and added the mixture. The result delighted them. They could drink fresh, clean water again.

As the end of the month drew near Paul went back to the bodies which had provided finance, spoke of the successful change which their money had produced and asked for more money. But this time their reply was: 'We gave you enough to test the remedy. It is up to the villagers themselves to pay for fresh supplies.'

But the villagers were too poor. So the water went back to its old state.

Both Jacques and Paul were angry with their older brother Claude who seemed to be doing nothing. He had chosen a shady spot by the main road by which people approached the village. There he meditated and talked to passers-by. Week after week passed and he did not so much as lend a hand to his brothers in their efforts.

One day when he came back at sundown, they got hold of him. 'Have you no feeling for the people and what they are suffering?' they asked. He gave no answer. 'Look,' they said again, 'we have tried this and that to make the water acceptable without success. What have you done?'

Claude replied quietly, 'The villagers will get good water.'

'It will be no thanks to you if they do,' said Jacques.

'Listen,' said Claude. 'Jacques, you encouraged the people to adjust their ways to the water just as it is. That was worth trying, though it was hard on the villagers. Paul, you looked for a cure. That was worth trying, though it proved too expensive. I argued that we could get no remedy that would last until we could get to the source of the springs – and that was out of reach. The thing to do was look for a fresh source.

'So I said to myself, "Why do people travel the road which leads to the village?" and answered, "some for business, some for pleasure: but also those who knew the village in older days and come back from time to time to visit relatives." I questioned these visitors.

'Today I met an old man who knew the place in bygone days. He told me of a large well which had once supplied hundreds of people with water for themselves and their crops. A sandstorm had got up and covered it. He remembered that, when that happened, the top was still on and it would thus be protected under the sand. People did not bother to dig it out because the springs we now use were nearer at hand. But we can dig – and get fresh water for everyone.'

Prayer:
Lord God,
Make us ready to learn from the wisdom of people in time past
as well as from those of today; that we may be able to take
from our planet what is needed to sustain life and still respect
the way it works, care for it as well as for ourselves, learning
how to leave it as an unspoiled birthright for our children's
children – as Jesus taught us to learn from flowers and ravens.
Amen.

Questions:
What did Jesus say about flowers and ravens? Hunt for an answer in Luke 12: 27–31. How can the history of Aboriginal peoples in Australia and the Americas help us to relate thoughtfully to our planet?

Sally and Susan

Sally and Susan were great friends. In their free time, they could be seen doing things together or just enjoying one another's company. They also had the same favourite sport, running. They would go out practising together. Then it would be: 'I'll race you to that tree or that fence!' and off they would go as fast as their legs would carry them. Almost always they would arrive at exactly the same time. But if you were there and looked carefully you might see that Sally eased up so that she would not be ahead

of Susan. It was different when it came to Sports Day. Sally always got ahead of Susan and won every time.

Sally's mum and dad were very proud of their daughter's success. They thought that she might one day become a great runner, maybe even reaching Olympic standards.

It was then that Sally's dad began to have a dream. In it he saw the two girls racing against each other. For the first part of the race neither had the advantage. Then Sally began to draw ahead. At that moment a burden appeared on Susan's back. She could not keep up with Sally because of the extra weight. So Sally always went on to win. But there was never a burden on Sally's back.

Sally's dad wondered and wondered what the dream could mean. He tried to puzzle it out himself without sharing it with his wife and the girls, but he could not make sense of it. Then one day he decided to go to Susan's home – something he had never done before. He met her mother. He did not want to ask what had happened to Susan's father in case it might open some old wounds. But he did not need to tell her mother of the dream. The house had damp walls. There was very little furniture. The money coming into the house each week could not have provided adequate meals for a healthy, growing lass. Bravely Susan's mum had scrimped and saved so that Susan could go to school wearing good clothes. But she could not give her a balanced diet as well. When it came to racing, Susan just did not have the strength that Sally had. She carried a burden which Sally was not asked to bear.

Susan's dad went home. This time he told his wife of his dream and what he had found. Together they discovered a way of secretly sharing some of their own income with Susan's mum. It was enough to make sure that Susan was properly fed each day. Once they had done that, the dream did not recur.

But after a short time, another dream took its place. There was Sally in a race. This time it was with children of every other race and colour and language in the whole world. They all set off together. Then Sally drew ahead of the others. But at the point at which Sally drew ahead he noticed that every other child had a ball and chain round a leg, holding them back.

When he woke he told his wife of the dream. 'There's no puzzle about the meaning this time,' she said. 'It isn't enough to help someone we know. So many of the world's children are disadvantaged. We have to fight to change the world so that everyone gets a chance in the race of life.'

From that time on, Sally's mum and dad became well known for their efforts to make sure that, all over the world, people could get clean water, good food, a chance in life – and not be burdened with debts which drag them back.

56

Prayer:
Lord God,
We praise and bless you that you have provided enough for all the people of the world to enjoy, as long as we share your gifts. You are loving and fair to all. Help us to live your way.
Amen.

Questions:
How should better-off people deal with those who are worse-off and how should better-off countries deal with worse-off countries which may suffer from hunger and be burdened with debt?

The Herbertson Family

The Herbertson children liked nothing better than to gather round their mum when she returned from one her journeys to Africa, to hear what she had been doing. It was a treat just to have her home. She had been trained in Development work and had kept up her skills as the children were growing up. Once Terry was 15 and Danny and Kathy were over 10 her husband Bruce and she had agreed to reverse family roles. He took a part-time job. The children shared in the cleaning of the house and the cooking. Their mum could then use her training and gifts for the benefit of disadvantaged countries in Africa.

'I've been asked at school what you do,' said Danny. 'I've said you're a kind of teacher – not of subjects but of ways of living.'

'And that you help people to make better use of resources

they already have,' chipped in Kathy.

'That's near enough a description of my work,' said mum, 'except that I am as much a learner as a teacher. I learn from the wisdom of local people.'

'You remember the area in Southern Africa where I thought that people were getting too little milk from their cows, and I imported one from Britain to improve the stock? Remember how I arranged a contest and how people were round-eyed as that cow out-milked first one, two, three and finally four of the native cows? I thought I had persuaded them to cross-breed. But one man who had been silent a long time spoke up. "I know your trick," he said. "What trick — there's no trick about it," I answered. "Oh yes," he said, "your cow die, no milk. Our cow die, three left." '

'When I went back this time I found he had been right. First the imported cow's yield dropped because the rough grass there did not have the same nourishment in it as had the grass here. Then, though we had doctored the cow against the tsetse fly and various diseases, it died. It had not been possible for it to absorb the protection the native cows had built into themselves over years and years.

'Do you remember what I told you about the Sahel?' mum then asked the children.

'Yes, you told us of it as a desert region, almost rainless,' said Terry. 'You were doing everything to help people in one area to improve their crops. You tried different seed, different strains of sorghum (the native crop), a coating for the grains which would protect them from local diseases. You helped the people make small catchment areas to keep what rain there was to irrigate the land. You introduced a hardy strain of goats, used to poor conditions. But nothing worked, did it? In the end you gave up, released the goats and withdrew.'

'Well remembered, Terry,' said his mum. 'Well, on this last journey I was in that region again. I went back to see how things were. The whole situation had improved! We had played our part making the small reservoirs. But nature did the rest. Wild ducks had landed there, the local people had tamed them and got eggs and food for the pot. The goats had adjusted to the new climate, had bred mightily in the wild; now the villagers had a whole herd which they had tamed afresh. Above all in importance was the harvest of sorghum.

'We had introduced varieties which gave much higher yields but the local people went back instead to forms of sorghum which their fathers and grandfathers had used. Although their harvests were much smaller they at least *had* harvests because the crops had an in-built ability to resist the worst of the climate which our so-called improved strains had not.

'People were making a living. We had helped them by being there – and had helped them even more by leaving them to work things out for themselves!'

59

Prayer:
Lord God,
What you give us you mean us to share.
Help us to appreciate one another's wisdoms.
Teach us when to make life better for others by going to their aid; and when to make life better by staying away and leaving them to it: that we may live as your family, giving and receiving.
Amen.

Question:
How can we find out when to go in and when to stay out of situations where help seems to be needed?

King Andreas
and Queen Felicia

Andreas, a king in a distant country, was all taken up with inventions. For his army he wanted the latest tanks, for his navy modern gunboats, for running the country from day to day the latest computers. He did not spend much time on the needs of people who longed for his companionship and friendship. It was how things worked and how they could be made to work better that took up his time from morning till night.

Then a friend of his late father, the ruler in another country, also died. He went to the funeral. There he met the ruler's daughter Felicia, an only child, who would thus succeed her father in governing the kingdom. She was young and very lively and vivacious, quick in mind and speech. Andreas was deeply attracted. A few months later he returned for her crowning. There was no doubt about it. He had fallen in love.

Shortly afterwards Felicia accepted an invitation to visit his kingdom. Full of excitement he showed her his weapons of war, scientific departments and industries, and laid them at her feet by asking her to marry him.

'Why?' she asked.

'Because I love you,' said Andreas, 'and with all this up-to-date equipment I can protect you, your household and country from any harm.'

But she refused him and returned to her own land.

Over the next few years other possible brides presented themselves. Some were more beautiful, some more wealthy than his first love. But just when he was on the point of offering them marriage, something held him back – a memory, a vision.

As the years went by, good tidings reached him from the kingdom of the young queen. She loved her people. She saw to it that the humblest were given a voice in the affairs of the kingdom. She honoured the poor and the old and made sure that they were provided for. As he heard of her way of life he began himself to think more of people and less of things. He started caring more for others and making sure that life was good for all his people, not just for those who were well off.

The longing to see the young queen again became stronger and stronger. He was afraid of another rebuff – but at last he plucked up courage to write asking if he might visit her and see her kingdom, of which he had heard so much good. He received a warm and welcoming invitation to do so.

She entranced him

more than ever. All he saw of her country delighted him. He kept alert to the possibility that he might have another chance to ask her hand in marriage. Then:

'Will you marry me?' she asked.

'Why?' he said, so taken aback that the words came out before he thought what he was saying.

'Because we have been in love all the time, haven't you noticed?' she replied.

'But I thought you did not feel that way. You refused me – why did you do so?'

'When you asked me to be your wife, you were all wrapped up in your own kingdom. You were almost like a child with toys you loved to see working. They were what took up your energy and time. But you have changed. People mean much more to you now. You have become a loving man. I want to marry that loving man.'

Prayer:
God the Lord,
You meant us to find how things work and how to make them work better.
You also meant us to learn how to love.
May knowing and loving go together in our lives.
Amen.

Questions:
Is it better to be able to make things work or to be loving human beings? Can the two go together?

Sylvia

Sylvia was 18 years old. She used to dream of distant places and longed to be able to go on holiday to explore some of them. Especially she dreamed of Sri Lanka. A travel programme on television about that country had thrilled her. How she wished that she could enjoy its white beaches, blue sea and swaying palms, and meet its smiling people. But the cost of travel was far beyond what she could afford.

Then in a magazine she saw a notice placed by a society which encouraged international friendships. With a beating heart she wrote to them and asked if there was someone about her own age in Sri Lanka with whom she could exchange letters. How delighted she was to be put in touch with Jeevani, also aged 18. She had been brought up in a village and had left it to work in a clothing factory in what was called a Free Trade Zone.

Sylvia wrote at once, telling Jeevani about the television programme which had aroused her interest. How attractive her homeland seemed to be, in contrast with Britain which had to endure so much rain and cold! She was sure that it must be lovely to live in Sri Lanka! Jeevani's answering letters surprised her. She did not speak of her own country in glowing terms and said nothing at all about her work. Instead she asked more and more about Britain as if it were a kind of Promised Land. When she did write about herself it was to tell of the village where she was brought up. People were poor but neighbours helped neighbours. It was almost as if she wished she had never left the village to work in the clothing factory. Something really good must have been in village life which she now missed. At this point the flow of letters from Jeevani to Sylvia came to a halt.

About then Sylvia had a birthday. Her mother gave her money to get a jacket which she knew Sylvia wanted. Sylvia got her best friend Doreen to go shopping with her. At two different shops they found a jacket of the right size and price, in the colour and style which suited her. Sylvia was torn between the two.

'Let's look at the labels and see where they were made,' said Doreen. One was made in Sri Lanka.

'That settles it,' said Sylvia. 'I will be helping Jeevani if I take this one.'

'The way I see it, said Doreen, 'it settles it the other way. For the sake of Jeevani you should not choose that one!'

Sylvia was puzzled. So Doreen explained: 'In the Free Trade Zone people like Jeevani can be made to work 14 hours per day. Wages are so low that seven or eight of the workers have to live together in one room in order to be able to afford the shelter it provides and the concrete floor on which they can lay their mats to sleep. They have to get water from a well and cook their own food after walking back from work – because there are so few buses. To buy the goods exported from the Zone is to encourage rich owners to take advantage of poor workers.' So Sylvia bought the other jacket. But she was still puzzled.

So she wrote to Jeevani asking if what Doreen had told her was true.

Jeevani replied that it was – but it must never be let known that she said so, or she might lose her job. The picture of Sri Lanka presented in glossy travel brochures showed the best of the country. There was a dark side as well. Now that Sylvia knew that, they could have an open and honest conversation in their letters.

Jeevani then apologized for the gap in her writing. At one

point she had been so tired, with the long working hours, that her hand had slipped on her sewing machine and a fingernail had been pierced by the needle. The finger had become infected and she had to be off work for several days, for which she got no pay. It was now healed enough for her to resume her letter-writing.

Sylvia wrote back and sympathized but said that Jeevani should have gone to her trade union representative. Jeevani replied that trade unions were officially allowed but in practice prevented from acting. She had no one to speak for her. If Sylvia wanted to help she should support fair trade policies promoted by such bodies as Christian Aid and Oxfam. Some firms teamed up with them when they insisted on fair working conditions. Only if factories passed that test would they buy the goods they offered.

'I see,' said Sylvia; 'it is not enough to look at the garment – we must also look at the label.'

'And ask whether those who produce the goods we buy are being fairly treated,' added Doreen.

Prayer:
Lord God,
Teach us to look beyond what first meets our eye and ask what lies behind it; lest other people suffer by thoughtless buying and selling when we shop.
Help us to do what we can to put right things which are wrong both in our own country and in other parts of the world.
Amen.

Questions:
Do you and your families look at the label and try to find out the conditions of work for those who produce what you buy? If not, what might you do in future?

Miss Mitchell

There may be no truth in the story that Leonardo da Vinci's maid saw his design for a flying machine on his drawing board and said, 'It looks fine; but what use is it?' But those words provided a starting point for Miss Mitchell and her class when they wanted to examine something more closely.

Miss Mitchell said to her class: 'Today it is my turn to choose our topic. I think I will choose "a forest": a forest looks nice, but what use is it? Please bring in some article tomorrow

CARING FOR PLANET EARTH

which suggests the usefulness of forests. I have won a box of sweets in a competition. That will be the prize for the most imaginative contribution in helping us to appreciate a forest.'

The next day the class brought in a weird assortment of things. Miss Mitchell wondered what on earth they all had to do with forests. She soon found out!

Richard's was a mystery parcel addressed to Miss Mitchell and labelled 'Handle with Care'. She unwrapped it and inside were a hatchet and a small saw to represent the big axes and powered chain saws which are used to cut down trees. 'We need wood for houses, furniture and fuel,' said Richard.

Suzanne brought an umbrella. 'A forest can provide shelter for animals and birds against winds and storms,' she said. 'It acts as a kind of umbrella.'

Mark brought a jar of bath crystals. 'What on earth do these have to do with forests?' asked Miss Mitchell. Mark replied gravely but politely, 'They represent silver iodide crystals with which aeroplanes "seed" clouds to make them produce rain. A forest's dark trees absorb the reflected light, produce a cool layer of air above it and that helps rain to fall.'

Ruth showed everyone her lunch box. 'A forest produces fruits, nuts and seeds to feed many living things,' she said.

Ronald had a small bag of earth tied tightly with string on the floor beside him. 'The roots of trees and vegetation on the floor of a forest bind the earth so that it is not blown away by the wind or washed away by rain. Silt in rivers raises flood levels. Winds can take away good fertile top soil,' he said.

Everyone was intrigued when Miriam produced a sponge. How could that be connected to a forest? 'Well,' she said, 'a forest is like a sponge. It absorbs water.' And as she spoke she dipped the sponge into a bowl of water. Then, lifting it out, she squeezed it gently. 'The forest also releases water slowly so that it does most good to the land around.' She went on: 'My uncle lives and works in China. Even the government there now realizes how short-sighted they were in cutting down so many forests. That was a major reason why they suffered massive floods. People were drowned or made homeless, livestock killed and vast areas of land have been made useless.'

By the time the bell went for the morning interval Miss Mitchell was really delighted with the progress made on the topic. So she took out the box of sweets, opened it, and handed it right round the class.

'You have given me new eyes,' she said. 'I will never look at a forest again without thinking about the many, many ways in which it plays a part in the life of the planet. You deserve to share the sweets.'

Prayer:

Lord God,
You have made a world in which everything depends on everything else.
Give us understanding so that we do not cause damage to some part of its life by thoughtless exploitation of another part.
Forgive the greed which makes people grab for immediate gain; and make us different, better people, we pray.
Amen.

Question:

The life of the planet may be mirrored in the life of a forest. Is it also a bit like a body, as described in 1 Corinthians 12: 12–26?

Kofi

Kofi had been blind and deaf from birth, but in his own way he was happy. He had his place to beg for food. People took pity on him and made sure that he got enough to get him through each day. Neighbours took him out in the morning and back at night. They had even worked out a language of touch which allowed them to speak with him.

He asked them about the world around and its people. They managed to get the information across that he asked for. They said that in the world there were important people who had more than enough, and unimportant people who mostly just managed to survive. Some of the unimportant ones could even starve to death: so he was lucky just to be able to keep going from one day to another.

One day the Healer arrived. He asked Kofi whether he wanted to be able to see. Eagerly he said that he did. The Healer put ointment on his eyes and laid hands on him in blessing. Sight began to come back to the eyes which had been sightless. The Healer went on his way.

It was some months later before the Healer returned to that place. As he drew near, he met a woman of the village and asked her how Kofi was getting on.

'Badly,' said the woman.

'Has he lost his sight again?' asked the Healer.

'He has recovered his sight completely, more's the pity!' came her reply.

'Why "more's the pity"?'

'When he was blind he was content. Now that he sees, he's questioning the way we live our lives. He says that people who have much more than they need are robbing those who are in want, taking more than their fair share of the world's goods. He also says that those kinds of people are not more important. The poor are every bit as important in God's sight. You found a man who was happy. See what you have done to him. He is now disturbed and angry.'

Not long after, the Healer again met Kofi who thanked him with shining eyes. The Healer, using the language of touch which the villagers had invented, asked him whether he wanted to be cured of his deafness. Kofi hesitated before answering. The world of sight had been a shock to him. But, in the end, he asked eagerly for further healing.

The Healer touched his ears with the fingers of both hands and laid hands on his head in blessing.

Hearing came back gradually, and the Healer went on his way.

It was again about a month or two before the Healer returned. This time a group ran towards him, clearly angry and upset. 'Was it not enough,' they asked, 'to rob a man of his peace, that you rob him of his faith as well?'

'What do you mean?' asked the Healer.

'Now that your patient can hear he has learned of other understandings of God, other explanations of the meaning of life.

'He no longer has something clear and definite to hold on to which can act as an anchor for his life. He has become restless. He distrusts the understanding of life which his forebears and we ourselves have handed on to him. He searches every form of belief, seeking a sure basis. He is a disturbance to us all.'

Just then Kofi spotted the Healer in the distance, ran to him and embraced him. The Healer turned to the group. Looking at Kofi he said, 'They tell me that I have robbed you of happiness and security by restoring your sight and hearing.'

'They have told you some part of the truth,' said Kofi. 'I am no longer the way I was. I no longer feel as secure as I was before. Only now I am alive.'

Prayer:
God the Lord,
Teach us not to be content to live in ignorance, but to accept the risk of seeing life as it truly is, to listen to discover the truth, however disturbing it may be, and to face up to the responsibilities of getting to know our whole planet, what is happening to it, and what we must do to care for it.
Amen.

Questions:
If you were blind and deaf but had a fairly comfortable life, would you want your sight and hearing back? If you got them back, would that not make life more difficult to cope with – why should you give yourself the hassle?

The Shield People

Since time began, the Shield People had swung through the heavens, diving and soaring, enjoying the freedom of the skies. Only when sunbeams danced in millions down the sun's rays did they put their shields in line to halt them.

'Why do you bar our way? We want to bring light to the earth,' the leading sunbeams protested. 'We want to give the earth warmth and fruitfulness,' said those behind them. 'We come to bring it health,' said the others.

The Shield People stood their ground. 'We will let enough of you pass to give living things light and warmth and health,' they said, 'but if we were to let you all pass you would blind people, melt ice till it drowns the land, cause skin cancers instead of giving fitness and health.'

'Who gave you the right to stop us?' asked the sunbeams.

'When God made the earth, we were set in place to guard and protect it,' answered the Shield People. 'We only keep out what will be harmful. The Universe is so big – you can dance through it for millions of years and never come to its end. So please go elsewhere.'

Millions of sunbeams got through to the people, the plants, the animals to give them life. Millions more were forced to dance away to other parts of the creation.

But then came a change! It was as if thunderbolts came through the atmosphere, hit the shields and broke off pieces. Through the breaks poured the sunbeams which were meant to go elsewhere. The earth came under threat. With pieces missing from their screen which had been set up to protect the planet, the Shield People could no longer do their work properly. 'Where', they wondered, 'did these thunderbolts come from?'

At first they suspected the sun. Was it annoyed because its children were being held back by the Shield People and many sent elsewhere? Was it trying to break down the barrier which filtered out harmful sunbeams? They kept a close watch on the sun. But it was not from that part of the Universe that the damage came.

Could it come from the earth? 'No way,' they thought. 'How could any earth creatures take action which led to them harming themselves?'

To make sure, they worked out a plan. 'Let the fastest of us come forward and catch some bolts before they reach the rest of us. We can then examine them for clues,' they decided. Flying at speed, risking their lives, some did just that.

'What does it say? What does it tell us?' asked the Shield People when the first one was caught.

'You'll find it hard to believe,' said the first catcher. 'It says, Made on Planet Earth'. As others were caught they were all found to bear the same label. Some bore the name 'Pollution', some 'Carbonic Acid Gas', some 'Greedy Exploitation'.

The Shield People looked at their broken and battered defences. 'We were trying to protect life on earth,' they said. 'Look how little the people care.'

'If they don't learn quickly their children will suffer,' said others.

'The whole planet will suffer,' they said with one voice.

Prayer:

God, Lord of the whole universe,
We confess that we have used the gift of planet earth carelessly
so that defences are destroyed which we should safeguard.
Help us to live differently, looking not only to our own
advantage but to the good of all living things.
Amen.

Question:

We use sun cream to protect ourselves against skin cancer: what
do we need to do to protect all creatures from 'planet-cancer'?